Support Helicopter Pilots

By Chris Oxlade

CRABTREE
Publishing Company
www.crabtreebooks.com

The World's MOST DANGEROUS Jobs

Author: Chris Oxlade
Managing editor: Paul Humphrey
Editorial director: Kathy Middleton
Editors: Rachel Tisdale, Adrianna Morganelli
Proofreader: Rachel Eagen
Series Design: Elaine Wilkinson
Page Design: sprout.uk.com
Cover design: Margaret Salter
Production coordinator: Margaret Salter
Prepress technician: Margaret Salter
Print coordinator: Katherine Berti

COVER STORY

◄ **COVER (top) – A military helicopter transports a jeep**

◄ **COVER (bottom) – Special forces unloading from a Chinook helicopter**

PAGE 1 – A Chinook helicopter comes into land following a mission

Photo credits:
Army.mil: page 22
Crown Copyright/MOD: pages 1 (POA Hamish Burke 2011), 6 (POA Tony Leather 2002), 7 (POA Tony Leather 2002), 9 (POA Hamish Burke 2011), 20 (POA Sean Clee 2006), 23 (James Stier)
Photoshot: page 27 (Imagebroker.net)
Shutterstock: Arie v.d. Wolde: cover (top); B747: cover (bottom);
U.S. Air Force: pages 5 (Senior Airman Noah R. Johnson), 8 (Senior Airman Nancy Hooks), 10-11, 13 (Staff Sgt. Brian Ferguson), 16, 17 (Airman 1st Class Benjamin Wiseman)
U.S. Air National Guard: page 19 (Airman 1st Class Jessica Green)
U.S. Army: page 18
U.S. Coast Guard: page 28-29 (Petty Officer 3rd Class Stephen Lehmann)
U.S. Navy: 12, 15 (Photographer's Mate 1st Class Martin Maddock), 25 (Mass Communication Specialist 1st Class Nathanael Miller)

Library and Archives Canada Cataloguing in Publication

Oxlade, Chris
    Support helicopter pilots / Chris Oxlade.

(The world's most dangerous jobs)
Includes index.
Issued also in electronic format.
ISBN 978-0-7787-5102-1 (bound).--ISBN 978-0-7787-5116-8 (pbk.)

    1. Helicopter pilots--Juvenile literature. 2. Aeronautics, Military--Juvenile literature. I. Title. II. Series: World's most dangerous jobs

UG631.O95 2012   j358.4   C2012-901569-5

Library of Congress Cataloging-in-Publication Data

Oxlade, Chris.
    Support helicopter pilots / Chris Oxlade.
        p. cm. -- (The world's most dangerous jobs)
    Includes index.
    Audience: Ages 8-11.
    ISBN 978-0-7787-5102-1 (library binding : alk. paper) -- ISBN 978-0-7787-5116-8 (pbk. : alk. paper) -- ISBN 978-1-4271-8073-5 (pdf) -- ISBN 978-1-4271-8077-3 (html)
    1. Military helicopters--Juvenile literature. 2. Helicopter pilots--Juvenile literature. I. Title.

    UG1230.O94 2012
    358.4'4--dc23
                                        2012008521

Crabtree Publishing Company

www.crabtreebooks.com   1-800-387-7650

Printed in Canada/042012/KR20120316

Published in Canada
Crabtree Publishing
616 Welland Ave.
St. Catharines, Ontario
L2M 5V6

Published in the United States
Crabtree Publishing
PMB 59051
350 Fifth Avenue, 59th Floor
New York, New York 10118

Published in the United Kingdom
Crabtree Publishing
Maritime House
Basin Road North, Hove
BN41 1WR

Published in Australia
Crabtree Publishing
3 Charles Street
Coburg North
VIC 3058

CONTENTS

Glossary words defined on p. 31 are in **bold** the first time they appear in the text.

FLYING SUPPORT HELICOPTERS

Imagine trying to control a big helicopter as it hovers over a desert. Its rotor is throwing up clouds of dust, making it hard for you to see the ground below. You can hear enemy gunfire close by. But you can't fly away. Heavily armed troops are clambering one by one into your helicopter, and it's your job to get them to safety! Flying support helicopters can be a risky business.

Carrying troops around is just one job for a support helicopter pilot. Support helicopters also ferry heavy equipment, such as guns and vehicles, re-supply troops with food and ammunition, carry out search-and-rescue missions and medical evacuations (**medevacs** for short), and **reconnaissance missions** to look for enemy positions.

Support helicopter pilots often fly over **combat zones**. But coming under enemy fire is just one danger of working as a support helicopter pilot. There's also bad weather, mountainous terrain, and the need to fly low and fast, often at night. Support helicopters do sometimes crash, and pilots are sometimes injured or killed. But flying a support helicopter is one of the most exciting, adventurous, and challenging jobs any pilot can do.

"But yeah, there are times when you wonder if you're going to make it back safe. And you know, you just keep going with the mission."

U.S. Army helicopter pilot

▼ Two HH-60G Pave Hawk support helicopters come in to land during a search-and-rescue mission.

▼ A British Royal Air Force (RAF) Chinook carries supplies to troops operating in the mountains of Afghanistan.

A Chinook's fuselage is big enough for 55 fully armed troops or 11 tons (10 metric tons) of cargo.

SUPPORT HELICOPTERS

Armies, navies, and air forces operate different support helicopters. The United States Army flies mainly CH-47 Chinooks and UH-60 Black Hawks. The British Royal Air Force flies mainly Chinook HC2s or HC3s and Merlin HC3s. These are some of the most advanced flying machines in the world.

Some supply helicopters are **single-rotor** helicopters. That means they have one main rotor on top. Very large supply helicopters, such as the Chinook, are **twin-rotor** helicopters. They have one rotor at the front and one at the rear. They can normally lift bigger loads than single-rotor helicopters. Most support helicopters have two engines. If one engine fails, the pilot can still land with the other.

Support helicopters have a big, empty **fuselage** for troops or **cargo**. Pieces of cargo too big for the fuselage, such as field guns, can be carried hanging underneath the helicopter.

Support helicopters normally have four crew members. There's the pilot and a co-pilot, who navigates and works the helicopter's weapons and defense systems. There are also **loadmasters**, who take care of passengers and cargo, and operate machine guns.

▲ This is the aircrew from a CH-47 Chinook helicopter.

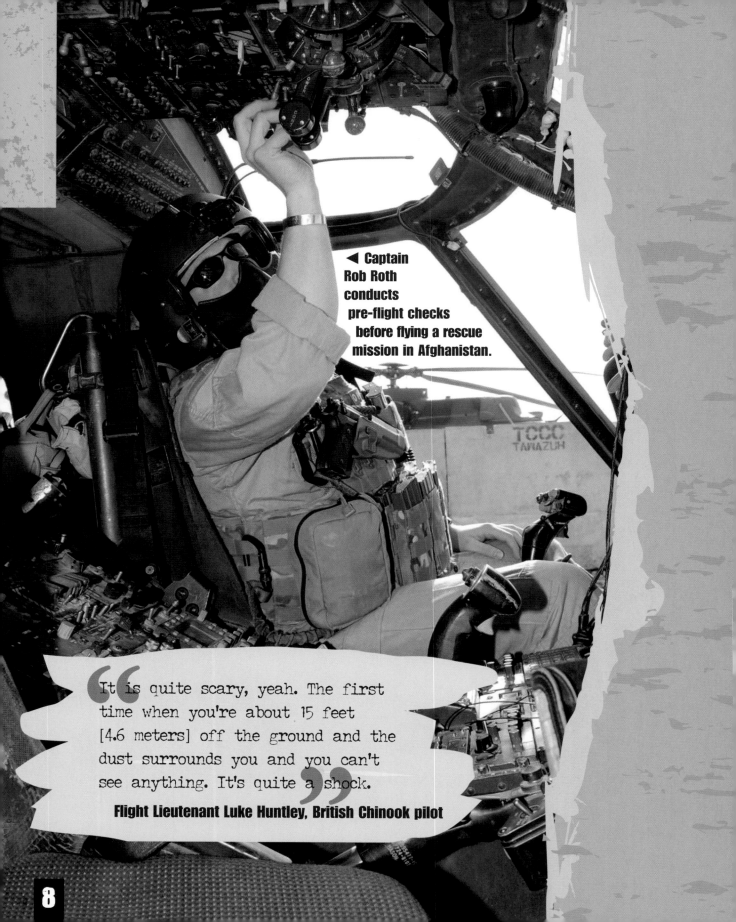

◄ Captain
Rob Roth
conducts
pre-flight checks
before flying a rescue
mission in Afghanistan.

"It is quite scary, yeah. The first
time when you're about 15 feet
[4.6 meters] off the ground and the
dust surrounds you and you can't
see anything. It's quite a shock."

Flight Lieutenant Luke Huntley, British Chinook pilot

THE DANGERS

A helicopter's spinning rotors make it more dangerous than flying a normal aircraft with fixed wings. A helicopter pilot has to adjust the controls all of the time or the helicopter could dive to the ground, or even flip right over. Engine problems or other mechanical failures can make a helicopter impossible to control. Flying too fast can also make a helicopter flip over. Support helicopter pilots say there is little margin for error in a helicopter—that means a pilot's mistake can easily cause a crash. In combat zones, where support helicopters are regularly shot at, most helicopter crashes are still caused by mechanical failure or human error.

The environment also makes flying helicopters dangerous. High winds, low cloud, fog, and snow make flying tricky. Support helicopters often operate in "hot and high" environments, such as hilly deserts. These are places where the air is warm and thin, which reduces engine performance, and where **dust storms** are regular. There's also the danger of hitting electricity poles and power lines. All of these dangers are worse for support helicopter pilots, as they willingly fly to rescue troops when other pilots might choose to stay on the ground, and are often flying under fire.

► A Royal Air Force Chinook helicopter returns from a mission and lands at Camp Bastion, Afghanistan.

TRAINING TO BE A PILOT

Before anyone can train to become a support helicopter pilot, they have to pass some physical tests. These include fitness tests, eyesight tests, and tests of hand-to-eye coordination. Pilot cadets learn the basics of flying in fixed-wing aircraft. As well as learning to control an aircraft, they learn about weather and navigation. Then they move on to flying helicopters. Taking off and landing are the most tricky things to learn.

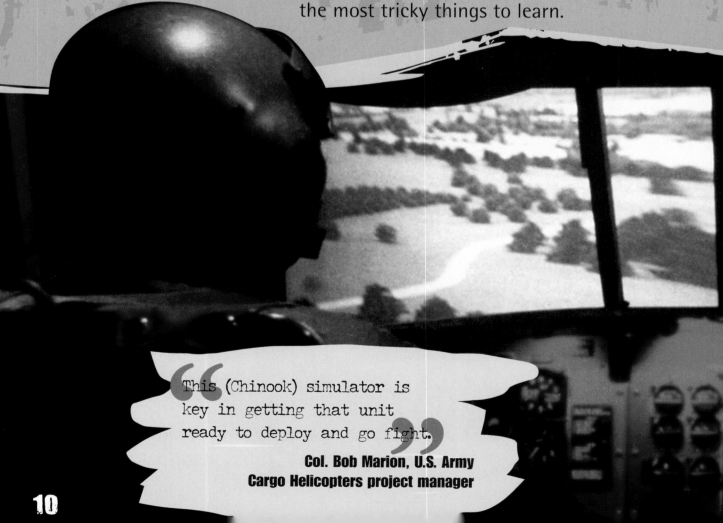

" This (Chinook) simulator is key in getting that unit ready to deploy and go fight. **"**

Col. Bob Marion, U.S. Army Cargo Helicopters project manager

After general helicopter training, pilots begin training on the type of support helicopter they are going to fly, such as the Chinook or Black Hawk. They learn about the controls and instruments, and how the helicopter flies. This is known as "conversion to type" training.

Trainee pilots also learn the special skills they will need to fly missions in support helicopters. These skills include flying using instruments, low flying, night flying, flying in combat zones, communications, and using a helicopter's weapons and defense systems. Pilots also practice what to do in emergencies, such as an engine failure. Much of this training is done in flight **simulators** instead of real helicopters.

▼ These pilots practice medium-lift capabilities in a Chinook flight-training simulator.

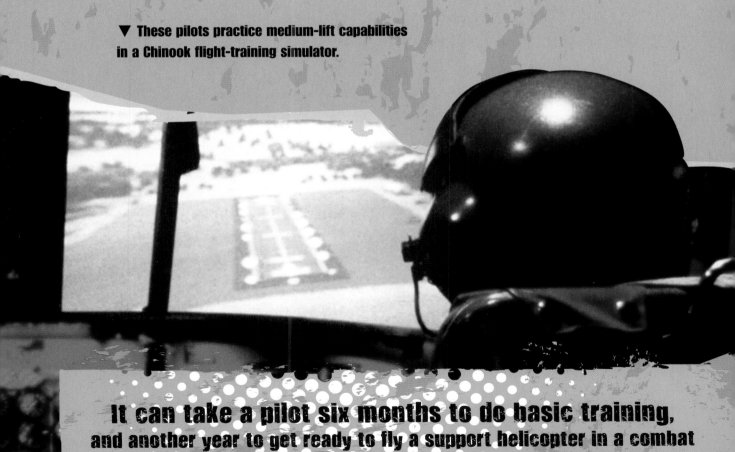

It can take a pilot six months to do basic training, and another year to get ready to fly a support helicopter in a combat zone. But helicopter pilots never really stop learning.

DAY-TO-DAY OPERATIONS

Support helicopter pilots spend months at a time working in combat zones. The time spent in a combat zone is called a tour of duty. On a tour of duty, pilots fly some missions regularly, carrying supplies of food and ammunition to fighting troops. They often fly these missions at night. Pilots must also be ready to fly emergency missions, such as evacuating or rescuing troops, or medical evacuations. As soon as a call comes into the helicopter base, the pilot and other crew members rush to their machine and take to the air. The pilots and their helicopters must be ready to fly at a moment's notice.

▼ Sea Knight helicopter pilots review a mission plan prior to take off.

Pilots always check the weather before they take off, as it could be dangerous to fly in bad weather. They plan a route to their destination to avoid enemy positions if they can. This reduces the chances of them being shot at. Before a mission to drop off troops, pilots study satellite photos of the landing site to make sure they know where to land. They also plan their journeys so they arrive at exactly the right time, which could be vital for the mission the troops are being sent on.

▼ A medevac helicopter waits for a civilian patient to be loaded on board by soldiers and crew.

LOW FLYING

Support helicopter pilots often fly very close to the ground, at full speed.

Pilots call this low flying. It's dangerous, but they actually do it to avoid even worse dangers. It's part of the job, and pilots train specially for it. When pilots low fly, they can be just 65 feet [20 meters] above the ground. They skim right over the roofs of houses. Even a small pilot error at this height could result in a crash. Pilots have to keep an eye out for obstacles such as electricity poles and power lines, too.

"Low flying is important to us on operations because it gives us the best tactical protection. It gives the enemy less time to react and shields us from potential firing points."

British support helicopter pilot

If low flying is so dangerous, why do pilots do it? The main reason is that it gives enemy soldiers on the ground less time to aim and fire at the helicopter with guns or grenade launchers. Enemy soldiers have only a couple of seconds to react when a helicopter comes into view, before it has disappeared again.

Low flying is even more risky in hilly countryside, where pilots have to keep changing height to stay low to the ground. This needs great skill and quick reactions. But low flying in hills does have advantages. Pilots can fly behind hills and down into valleys to hide from enemy attackers.

▼ A Sea Stallion helicopter flies low over Greek terrain, as the crew survey the land during a military exercise.

NIGHT FLYING

Support helicopter pilots try to avoid being spotted by the enemy, so that the enemy soldiers don't have a chance to attack them. The best way to avoid being seen is to fly at night, when it's dark. This is known as night flying. You can imagine the dangers of flying a helicopter at night.

At night, pilots can't see where they are going. They depend on their navigational instruments.

"En route to target the ambient light levels were so poor that even our NVGs [night-vision goggles] struggled to provide much more than a dark green nothingness."

Flight Lieutenant Chris Hasler, British Chinook pilot

▲ A Black Hawk helicopter flies a night mission over Baghdad, Iraq.

Pilots fly safely at night using their instruments. They have instruments that show if the helicopter is flying level, climbing or descending, and instruments that tell them where they are, how high they are, and how fast they are going. Pilots also fly at low level at night. This is only possible when they wear night-vision goggles (NVGs). These create an image by detecting heat from the landscape. Warm things, such as vehicle engines and people, look bright, and cold things look dark. Pilots often find their landing zones at night by homing in on flares set off by troops on the ground.

◄ This pilot finishes a pre-flight check prior to take off on a search-and-rescue night-time mission.

AVOIDING DANGER

Support helicopter pilots do their best to keep themselves, their helicopters, their crew, their passengers, and their cargo out of danger. For enemy soldiers, a helicopter is a valuable target. They know that destroying a helicopter, or even forcing it to make an emergency landing, will disrupt an army's movement of troops, equipment, and supplies, making it harder for the army to fight. A support helicopter is also easier to shoot down than other aircraft because of its large size. Enemy soldiers attack helicopters with small-arms (such as rifles and machine guns), anti-aircraft guns, rocket-propelled grenades, and sometimes with **surface-to-air (SAM) missiles**.

▼ **Two CH-47 Chinook helicopters fly in convoy to avoid danger.**

Pilots fly low to the ground to make it hard for enemy soldiers to target them, and they fly at night so they are difficult to see. They also stay on the ground for the shortest possible time in danger zones, because this is when they are most at risk. Pilots also regularly change routes so that the enemy can't easily guess where they are going next. Support helicopters also fly together to protect each other, and sometimes with attack helicopter escorts.

Support helicopters have armor.
The Black Hawk's armor can stop 23-mm shells from an anti-aircraft gun. Pilots' seats are also armored, and pilots wear body armor and helmets.

"Helicopters have got ballistic protection, but you can't armor the whole thing, or it would never take off."

John Pike, American defense expert

▲ Two Pave Hawk rescue helicopters fly in convoy on a training mission.

UNDER FIRE

We've seen how pilots try to avoid being shot at, but what can they do when they actually *are* attacked? How can they avoid damage to the helicopter, or even being shot down?

For a start, helicopter crews can fire back. Support helicopters are armed with machine guns, normally in the doorways. Pilots can also take **evasive** action. That means flying randomly up and down and from side to side to make the helicopter a more difficult target.

▲ The pilot of this Chinook releases decoy flares on a mission in Afghanistan.

The most dangerous weapon for helicopters are surface-to-air missiles (SAMs). These high-speed missiles detect heat from a helicopter's engines and fly toward them. Support helicopters have **radar** systems that spot the missiles coming and warn the pilots. Pilots can then defend against a SAM by firing flares from the helicopter. With luck, the missile will follow a hot flare and miss the helicopter.

Pilots can avoid being spotted by enemy radar by dropping strips of metal foil called chaff. The radar sees the chaff, so the helicopter can hide and escape.

Sometimes helicopters are hit and damaged, so they can't continue on flying. Then the pilot tries to make a controlled landing without crashing. Sometimes a crash is unavoidable. Pilots don't call a crash a crash; they call it an uncontrolled descent into terrain.

" And then I saw the hole in the windscreen and I thought, uh huh, I think I've just been hit in the head! And then came a feeling of elation, of I think I've just been shot in the head and I've survived — well, good stuff! "

Flight Lieutenant Ian Fortune, British Chinook pilot

DROP OFF AND PICK UP

The most dangerous time for a support helicopter pilot is landing to drop off or pick up troops or equipment. That's because helicopters are an easy target when they are moving slowly. Pilots try to spend as little time as possible on the ground.

In hills or mountains, there's often nowhere flat for pilots to land their helicopters. Instead of landing, they hover just above the ground, or with one wheel on the ground, so that troops can jump out or clamber in.

▲ A Chinook support helicopter drops off troops.

Chinook pilots have a special trick to pick up marines in inflatable boats. They hover with the helicopter's rear ramp in the sea so the boats can be driven up the ramp and into the fuselage. Maneuvers like this need great piloting skills. Often a pilot can't see how close the helicopter is to the landing surface. They rely on the crew to call precise instructions to them.

"For us, the objective was to get the infantry on the ground where they wanted to be at, at a particular time. And then we usually get a little bit of background of exactly what they're going to do on the ground, so we can help them do their mission. But, for us, the objective is always get them on, on target, plus or minus 165 feet [50 meters], plus or minus 30 seconds."

John Pike, American defense expert

▶ A Merlin HC3 helicopter drops an underslung load during a training exercise in the Californian desert.

HELICOPTERS AT SEA

Navies around the world fly support helicopters from aircraft carriers and other warships. Pilots fly these helicopters on reconnaissance missions, to carry supplies between ships and to troops on land, and to carry wounded soldiers to hospital ships. For example, U.S. Navy pilots fly MH-53 Sea Stallion helicopters to detect and clear mines at sea, and Super Stallions to transport marines and heavy cargo. They also fly CH-46 Sea Knights to support troops in combat zones on land.

Ship-based transport helicopters are used when an army does not have a base on land from where it can fly its helicopters.

Flying helicopters from the decks of ships brings extra dangers for pilots. The take-off and landing area they use on deck is very small. Take-off and landing is tricky enough when the sea is calm. When it is rough the deck rolls from side to side and moves up and down. Pilots have to slam their helicopters onto the deck to avoid bouncing off again and possibly toppling into the sea.

▶Aviation crew members direct a Pave Hawk helicopter, as its pilot concentrates during take off from the USS *Ponce* during training exercises.

DISASTER RELIEF

Support helicopter pilots normally work in combat zones. But sometimes they are called to help when natural disasters strike. Larger countries, such as the United States, Canada, and the United Kingdom, often lend helicopters and pilots to other countries to help after natural disasters.

Natural disasters include floods, hurricanes, earthquakes, and famines, which often leave people trapped in buildings or on small patches of dry land, or without clean water, food, and shelter. The first job for support helicopter pilots is to rescue people. Pilots can hover to pluck people to safety, or land on small patches of dry land to pick people up.

Lines of communication, such as roads and railways, can be damaged, so trucks and trains can't carry emergency supplies to affected people. Helicopters are sometimes the only way of getting supplies, such as fresh water, food, emergency shelters, and medicines, from disaster relief bases to towns and villages that are cut off. Sometimes the helicopters carry supplies from ships.

▶ This helicopter delivers relief items used for shelter to victims in the Palas Valley, Pakistan, following the earthquake in 2005.

Flying helicopters for disaster relief needs the same skills as flying in combat zones. It's dangerous, too. During some disasters the weather can be bad. And sometimes natural disasters happen where there's a war going on, and pilots trying to help out can be shot at.

> "If it hadn't been for these helicopters, about 600 people in my village who survived would surely have died.
>
> **Abdul Ghafoor, resident of Chikothi, Pakistan, after the earthquake in 2005**

AIR-SEA RESCUE

Support helicopter pilots also fly
helicopters that rescue people at sea
and in hazardous places on land, such as mountains. These
helicopters are called air-sea rescue helicopters. They are
normally operated by air forces and navies. They
sometimes rescue military pilots who have ditched their
aircraft in the sea, but they help anybody who is in trouble.

Air-sea rescue helicopters pluck people from the decks of sinking ships, carry sick or injured sailors to hospital, rescue swimmers who have been swept out to sea, lift sick and injured people from mountains and cliffs, and help people trapped by floods.

Only the most skilled support helicopter pilots fly air-sea rescue helicopters. They have to fly very accurately. For example, one day an air-sea rescue pilot might have to hover over a sinking ship in a fierce storm, while a crew member lowers down to the ship by **winch**. The next day he or she might have to fly within a few meters of a cliff face in a strong wind to rescue an injured mountaineer.

Flying over the sea is risky for helicopter pilots. If a helicopter breaks down it has nowhere to land but in the sea. The pilots and other crew members wear life jackets, special survival suits that keep them warm in cold water, and emergency beacons in case they end up in the water. They practice escaping from a sinking helicopter as part of their training.

◄▼ A U.S. Coast Guard Jayhawk helicopter hovers above two rescue swimmers during a search-and-rescue training exercise.

IT'S A FACT!

It takes around two and a half years in total to train to become a helicopter support pilot. This is one of the longest training programs in the armed forces.

The Merlin helicopter has the capacity to carry 16 stretchers for casualty evacuation.

The UH-60 Blackhawk helicopter can move a 105mm Howitzer, all six crew members, and 30 rounds of ammunition in a single trip.

The HC2 Chinook can carry two Land Rovers, 55 troops, or 11 tons (10 metric tons) of freight. It also has three cargo hooks, which means it can carry multiple external

The rotor span of a Chinook helicopter is 60 feet (18 meters).

The Sea King search and rescue team is ready to fly in 15 minutes during daylight hours and 45 minutes at night.

Support Helicopters Online
www.airforce.com
www.raf.mod.uk

GLOSSARY

cargo A load of something

chaff Strips of metal foil that pilots drop to avoid being detected on enemy radar

combat zone An area where fighting is taking place

dust storm A strong, hot dry wind, full of dust

evasive Avoiding an attack. Pilots can fly up and down and from side to side to avoid being an easy target

fuselage The main body of a support helicopter; the area where troops and cargo are carried

loadmaster A member of a support helicopter crew who takes care of passengers and cargo, and operates machine guns

medevac Short for medical evacuation.

night-vision goggles Goggles worn by pilots and soldiers to enable them to see in the dark

radar Technology that uses reflected radio waves to detect, locate, and track objects

reconnaissance mission A mission to explore an area to gather information

simulator A machine designed to reproduce the essential features of flying. Pilots use simulators to practice during their training

single-rotor Describes a helicopter with one rotor

surface-to-air missiles (SAMs) Weapons that are fired from the ground against a target in the air

twin-rotor Describes a helicopter with two rotors

winch A machine for lifting loads

INDEX